Strategic Studies Institute
and
U.S. Army War College Press

EUROPEAN MISSILE DEFENSE AND RUSSIA

Keir Giles
with
Andrew Monaghan

July 2014

*****

*****

Comments pertaining to this report are invited and should be forwarded to: Director, Strategic Studies Institute and U.S. Army War College Press, U.S. Army War College, 47 Ashburn Drive, Carlisle, PA 17013-5010.

*****

This manuscript was funded by the U.S. Army War College External Research Associates Program. Information on this program is available on our website, *www.StrategicStudies Institute.army.mil,* at the Opportunities tab.

*****

*****

The Strategic Studies Institute and U.S. Army War College Press publishes a monthly email newsletter to update the national security community on the research of our analysts, recent and forthcoming publications, and upcoming conferences sponsored by the Institute. Each newsletter also provides a strategic commentary by one of our research analysts. If you are interested in receiving this newsletter, please subscribe on the SSI website at *www.StrategicStudiesInstitute.army.mil/newsletter.*

FOREWORD

The recent history of the conversation with Russia over plans for European missile defense has been one of repeated and unsuccessful attempts to allay strongly worded Russian concerns. None of these attempts has mitigated Russia's trenchant opposition to U.S. plans. At times, this opposition can appear based on grounds which are spurious or incomprehensible.

In this monograph, Mr. Keir Giles, a British academic and long-term scholar of Russia, examines the history of missile defense, and the current dialogue, from a Russian perspective in order to explain the root causes of Russian alarm. He presents specific recommendations for managing the Russia relationship in the context of missile defense. Important conclusions are also drawn for the purpose of managing the dialogue over missile defense plans not only with Russia as an opponent, but also with European North Atlantic Treaty Organization allies as partners and hosts. The latter are especially significant in the light of these partners' heightened hard security concerns following Russian annexation of Crimea and continuing hostile moves against Ukraine.

This monograph was completed before the start of Russia's annexation of Crimea in March 2014, but already warned of the prospect of direct military action by Russia in Europe to protect Moscow's self-perceived interests. Given the continuing hostility of Russian messaging over U.S. missile defense plans, the Strategic Studies Institute strongly recommends this monograph to policymakers contributing not only to missile defense planning, but also to any aspect of policy affecting the defense of Europe.

DOUGLAS C. LOVELACE, JR.
Director
Strategic Studies Institute and
  U.S. Army War College Press

ABOUT THE AUTHORS

KEIR GILES is the director of the Conflict Studies Research Centre (CSRC), a group of deep subject matter experts on Eurasian security formerly attached to the United Kingdom (UK) Ministry of Defence. Now operating in the private sector, CSRC provides in-depth analysis on a wide range of security issues affecting Russia and its relations with overseas partners. After beginning his career working with paramilitary aviation in Russia and Ukraine immediately following the fall of the Soviet Union, Mr. Giles joined the BBC Monitoring Service (BBCM) to report on political and military affairs in the former Soviet space. While attached from BBCM to CSRC at the UK Defence Academy, he wrote and briefed for UK and North Atlantic Treaty Organization (NATO) government agencies on a wide range of Russian defense and security issues. Uniquely, he is a double Associate Fellow of the Royal Institute of International Affairs (Chatham House) in London, UK, as well as a regular contributor to research projects on Russian security issues in both the UK and Europe. Mr. Giles's work has appeared in a wide range of academic and military publications across Europe and in the United States.

ANDREW MONAGHAN is a Research Fellow in the Russia and Eurasia Programme at Chatham House and an Academic Visitor at St. Antony's College, Oxford, UK. Additionally, he is the Founder and Director of the Russia Research Network, an independent organization for the generation of information and expertise on Russian politics, security, and economic issues based in London. In this capacity, he has served as an expert witness to the House of Commons Foreign Affairs Select Committee. Until late-2012, Dr. Monaghan directed Russian related research in the Research Division of the NATO Defense College in Rome, Italy. In this role, he was also the senior researcher on energy security matters. Prior to that, he held positions as a Senior Research Associate at the Advanced Research and Assessment Group, part of the Defence Academy of the UK, and a Visiting Lecturer in the Defence Studies Department of King's College, London, the civilian academic arm of the Joint Services Command and Staff College at the Defence Academy. Dr. Monaghan holds an M.A. in war studies and a Ph.D. in Russian foreign policy (Russian perspectives of Russia-European Union security relations) from the Department of War Studies, King's College.

SUMMARY

When U.S. President Barack Obama cancelled a scheduled September 2013 summit meeting with his Russian counterpart, Vladimir Putin, "lack of progress on issues such as missile defense" was cited as the primary justification. Despite widespread and well-founded assumption that the real trigger for the cancellation was the Russian decision to offer temporary asylum to Edward Snowden, the citing of missile defense was indicative. The comment marked one of the periodic plateaus of mutual frustration between the United States and Russia over U.S. attitudes to missile defense capability, stemming from a continued failure to achieve meaningful dialogue over U.S. plans and Russian fears.

Russia's vehement objections to U.S. plans for missile defense installations in Europe, and the range of unfriendly actions promised in response, are often portrayed as irrational, the arguments technically flawed, the behavior deliberately obstructive, and the underlying threat perception hopelessly out of date. Yet an examination of the missile defense relationship between Russia and the United States over time shows that the fundamental Russian concerns stem from ideas of state security which, while discounted elsewhere, remain valid in the Russian security calculus. The fundamentally different weight and importance attached by Russia to nuclear weapons as both a guarantee and a symbol of statehood can be challenging for U.S. observers to grasp, but it is critical to understanding those Russian statements that do not, at first sight, make rational sense to U.S. policymakers. Furthermore, while the current Russian proposals for compromise—at least those stated in public—are wholly unrealistic, bear in mind that some of the security considerations behind them, at various times, have been both shared and voiced by the United States.

This monograph will examine the historical precedents for the current missile defense impasse, in order to explain the Russian attitude, and draw conclusions about both the most recent developments in the conversation between the United States and Russia and its likely further progress and prospects, if any, for a resolution.

EUROPEAN MISSILE DEFENSE AND RUSSIA

Keir Giles
with
Andrew Monaghan

INTRODUCTION

When U.S. President Barack Obama cancelled a scheduled September 2013 summit meeting with his Russian counterpart, Vladimir Putin, "lack of progress on issues such as missile defense" was cited as the primary justification.[1] Despite widespread and well-founded assumption that the real trigger for the cancellation was the Russian decision to offer temporary asylum to Edward Snowden, the citing of missile defense was indicative. The comment marked one of the periodic plateaus of mutual frustration between the United States and Russia over U.S. attitudes to missile defense capability, stemming from a continued failure to achieve meaningful dialogue over U.S. plans and Russian fears.

Russia's vehement objections to U.S. plans for missile defense installations in Europe, and the range of unfriendly actions promised in response, are often portrayed as irrational, the arguments technically flawed, the behavior deliberately obstructive, and the underlying threat perception hopelessly out of date.[2] Yet, an examination of the missile defense relationship between Russia and the United States over time shows that the fundamental Russian concerns stem from ideas of state security which, while discounted elsewhere, remain valid in the Russian security calculus. The fundamentally different weight and importance attached by Russia to nuclear weapons as both

1

a guarantee and a symbol of statehood can be challenging for U.S. observers to grasp, but it is critical to understanding those Russian statements that do not, at first sight, make rational sense to U.S. policymakers. Furthermore, while the current Russian proposals for compromise—at least those stated in public—are wholly unrealistic, bear in mind that some of the security considerations behind them, at various times, have been both shared and voiced by the United States.

This monograph will examine the historical precedents for the current missile defense impasse in order to explain the Russian attitude and draw conclusions about both the most recent developments in the conversation between the United States and Russia, and its likely further progress and prospects, if any, for a resolution.

DÉJÀ VU ALL OVER AGAIN: MISSILE DEFENSE IN THIS CENTURY AND THE LAST

Topical reporting on missile defense discussions between Russia and the United States often gives the impression that the issue is a new one, and has only been a significant factor in the bilateral relationship since the late-2000s and the announcement of the first round of plans for U.S. ballistic missile defense installations in Poland and the Czech Republic.[3] In fact, the problem has a long history through various cycles of missile defense initiatives by both the United States and the Soviet Union over previous decades. Examining the history of missile defense systems on both sides is instructive, since many arguments over their strategic implications are repeated decades apart, and there are precedents from Soviet times which reveal an entirely consistent Russian approach to the problem over time—as well as an inconsistent and unpredictable U.S. approach.

As expressed by Dmitry Medvedev during his term as Russian president: "Russia's relations with the USA and the North Atlantic Treaty Organization (NATO) in the missile defense area have a long and complicated history."[4] This history needs to be considered from both the U.S. and Soviet sides, because it helps provide a framework for understanding the current Russian objections and points to likely future developments in the Russian stance. It will also show that some of the Russian objections to U.S. plans, which are perceived as irrational by the current U.S. leadership, in fact, precisely mirror U.S. statements and attitudes from previous decades.

Early Days.

Interest in development of a ballistic missile defense (BMD) system first arose in the United States during World War II, when observing the British experience of being subjected to ballistic missile attack from Germany and considering the future implications for the United States.[5] BMD development accelerated in the late-1950s, when successful Soviet intercontinental ballistic missile (ICBM) launches, combined with aggressive Soviet expansionism, accentuated U.S. vulnerability. The Cuban Missile Crisis in October 1962 highlighted the lack of available defensive measures against missile attack—but the outcome of the crisis, and the resulting partial strategic setback for the Union of Soviet Socialist Republics (USSR), caused the Soviet Union to put greater emphasis on its own antimissile systems. Reports of the planned Soviet BMD system, in turn, caused then-U.S. President Lyndon

Johnson to authorize the Sentinel system, designed to defend the U.S. homeland against a light missile attack, in September 1967.[6] Thus the pattern was set for the reactive, interdependent nature that U.S. and Russian missile defense plans have retained ever since.

President Richard Nixon refocused U.S. missile defense so the Sentinel system would protect U.S. deterrent forces as opposed to the general population, and the concept was developed into a layered defense system and renamed Safeguard. At the same time, recognition on both sides of the destabilizing potential of missile defense systems led to agreement that the Strategic Arms Limitation Talks (SALT), beginning in 1969, would include discussions on limiting missile defense. The result was the signing of the Anti-Ballistic Missile (ABM) Treaty in 1972 by President Nixon and General Secretary of the Central Committee of the Communist Party of the Soviet Union Leonid Brezhnev, simultaneously with an Interim Agreement on strategic offensive arms limitations.[7] The implication that the offensive and the defensive are inseparable in strategic stability is a theme that is still relevant to Russian objections to U.S. missile defense plans today, and will be discussed further.

The ABM Treaty limited the number of BMD sites that each side could maintain; a 1974 protocol to the treaty further reduced the sites on each side from two to one.[8] Of these two possible sites, only the Soviet one was fully implemented. The U.S. Safeguard system was cancelled by Congress in 1975, because of doubts over its effectiveness, vulnerability, and cost. In addition, the state of interception technology at the time dictated that the interceptor missiles should be nuclear armed to ensure a kill. As explained by Finnish physicist and prominent defense researcher Stefan Forss, this was to some extent self-defeating:

> Exploding a nuclear-tipped interceptor in the upper atmosphere creates plasma that radar waves are not able to penetrate. Accordingly, the battle management radar is likely to go 'blind' after the first interceptor is used, and follow-on missiles cannot be engaged. The BMD system is essentially reduced to a single shot system.[9]

In addition, the implications of detonating friendly nuclear missiles over U.S. population centers gave rise to a degree of concern.[10] The Soviet leadership, meanwhile, was unencumbered by democratic oversight of its defense planning, and the USSR continued development and implementation of its nuclear-armed A-35 BMD installations around Moscow, descendents of which continue in service today. Thus, it can be argued that, although the aim of the ABM Treaty was to maintain strategic stability, this aim was not achieved due to the resulting imbalance of only one side, the USSR, implementing BMD capability.[11] The Soviet Union, therefore, had cause to be entirely satisfied with the ABM Treaty. This is significant when considering both Russian objections to its eventual cancellation in 2002 and earlier Soviet responses to the next cycle in the BMD game: Strategic Defense Initiative (SDI).

Strategic Defense Initiative.

By the early-1980s, the United States had begun to worry that the Soviets had achieved a first strike capability that would allow them to cripple U.S. strategic forces and still maintain enough nuclear weapons to destroy America's cities. This situation led President

Ronald Reagan to place greater emphasis on developing missile defenses. In March 1983, Reagan gave a speech that launched SDI and promised what was widely quoted as "Star Wars" technology. Despite the careful wording of the speech, and mention of consistency with U.S. obligations under the ABM Treaty, it contained phrases that were deeply alarming to the Soviet leadership, since the promise to "eliminate the threat posed by nuclear weapons" by rendering them "impotent and obsolete" implied that the Soviet deterrent threat would be neutralized, destroying the foundations of strategic stability as understood by both sides at the time, and leaving the USSR vulnerable to nuclear attack without the possibility of retaliation.[12] According to then Soviet leader Yuri Andropov, who, like his successor Vladimir Putin, had moved into a leadership position from a role as head of the country's intelligence organization, this deliberate destabilization was "not just irresponsible, [but] insane."[13]

The Soviet response to SDI needs to be considered, because it is a direct precursor to Russian responses to current U.S. BMD plans. Three issues of serious concern to the Russian leadership today directly echo the situation 30 years ago. First, the concern over the development of technology that eventually may limit the effectiveness of the Russian nuclear deterrent, or indeed render it useless — as in 1983, the technology and level of implementation is not currently a threat to the Russian deterrent, but extensive future development is promised by the U.S. side, with no stated limit on the planned capability. Second, and related, nuclear weapons held and still hold a very different place in the security calculus, and indeed in the national identity, of the Soviet Union and Russia, rendering their devaluation a much less desirable end result than it is for the United States and many other states. Finally, Soviet efforts to ensure the maintenance of strategic stability by investing even more heavily in defense are widely credited with accelerating the economic collapse of the Soviet Union and its subsequent disappearance as a state—an existential threat of which the Russian leadership is acutely conscious, and keen not to repeat.[14] All these issues remain current and will be considered further in subsequent discussion of the current Russian stance on U.S. BMD plans.

Exit the USSR.

In late-1989, the administration of President George H. Bush initiated a review of the SDI program as part of a broader examination of U.S. strategic requirements for the "new world order" that was thought to be emerging. Responding to the change in the nature of the ballistic missile threat that was highlighted by missile attacks on Israel during the Gulf war in 1990, President Bush announced in 1991 that the Defense Department was refocusing the SDI program from defense against a massive Soviet missile attack to greater emphasis on intercepting limited strikes.

The collapse of the Soviet Union at the end of that year appeared to vindicate this shift in U.S. policy. The United States and its allies pursued an energetic program in the early-1990s to ensure that former Soviet nuclear capabilities were concentrated in Russian hands rather than scattered across several newly independent republics. But thereafter, throughout the rest of that decade and into the new millennium, in its public statements, the United States largely ignored the possibility of deliberate targeting by Russian nuclear capability and focused instead on proliferation of ballistic missiles to rogue nations and, potentially, terrorist organizations. U.S. missile defense technologies and concepts were adapted to meet a new and growing threat: a possible limited conventional or nuclear attack on U.S. territory by ballistic missiles from rogue states or even nonstate actors. Guarding against this eventuality continues to shape much of U.S. policy on BMD today; but, crucially, it does so to a degree that Moscow does not fully understand, since Russia does not fully share this threat assessment.

Accompanying this shift in emphasis was the development of new interceptor technology, for the first time making kinetic hit-to-kill capability a realistic prospect instead of relying on warheads with either nuclear or conventional explosives to achieve destruction by an explosion in proximity to the incoming missile. With this new capability, mid-flight interceptions became possible, with much reduced concern over collateral damage or environmental effects. While the perceived benefits from the U.S. side were clear, the development of more ecologically friendly interceptors was of limited comfort to Russia: the same technological improvements removed the nuclear single-shot problem and made BMD a credible option for the United States.

During the same period, Russia moved almost overnight from a comfortable position of strong conventional deterrence through the massive superiority of troop numbers of the Soviet Army to a reliance on nuclear missiles as the only effective deterrent, at strategic or other levels, which was available to the newly emergent Russian Federation. According to President Putin, speaking in 2006, the entire Russian army had to be stripped of its combat-capable units and personnel in order to mount the limited campaign in Chechnya at the end of 1994.[15] Throughout the following decade, Russian defense budgets continued a relative decline, with funding priority going to the nuclear forces. While perceived as being of limited relevance by the United States and its allies, none of whom intended to attack Russia, the Russian leadership believed these nuclear forces constituted the last-ditch guarantee of Russian sovereignty and protection of its fundamental interests. Furthermore, throughout the worst period of budgetary meltdown and economic implosion, Russia continued investment in development of its own anti-missile capabilities—albeit with apparently limited results. These capabilities were seen as critical to maintaining nuclear parity, and nuclear parity in turn was seen as critical to guaranteeing Russian state interests and, indeed, the continued existence of the state itself.

Thus the situation throughout the late-1990s provides another example pertinent today. Russia not only perceives itself to be vulnerable to military attack from the United States due to a severe conventional capability gap, but it also proceeds from an assessment of this capability to include in its security planning the possibility of such an attack taking place. This consideration can be either imperfectly understood or disregarded by sections of the U.S. policymaking community—and therefore Russian concerns are heightened by U.S. actions that are, in fact, unrelated to Russia. The pattern continues today that deterrent messages from the United States, which are intended for a specific audience far away from Russia, are treated by the Russians as "to whom it may concern," triggering a reaction that occasionally surprises the United States, and particularly those sections of its leadership that had forgotten Russia was there.

9

The United States Pulls Out of the ABM Treaty.

From the Russian perspective, the situation after 2001 deteriorated still further. On December 13, 2001, President George W. Bush gave Russia a 6-month notice of U.S. intent to withdraw from the ABM Treaty so that the United States could pursue development of the program at that time known as National Missile Defense (NMD) — already under way, in potential violation of U.S. treaty obligations. But despite the significance of the withdrawal, which undermined Russia's entire concept of strategic stability, the official response from Russia was measured and muted, in sharp contrast to the heated rhetoric that greeted subsequent U.S. BMD initiatives. President Putin restricted himself to calling the withdrawal "mistaken" and referred to Russian capabilities for overcoming BMD systems in an almost conciliatory manner rather than the threatening tone that similar statements took on subsequently.[16]

The reasons behind this contrast need to be examined, as they may suggest means of attenuating hostile Russian reactions, and the transactional costs they entail, in the future. First, this occurred at the peak of strategic cooperation between the United States and Russia following the September 11, 2011 (9/11) attacks: cooperation that Bush referred to as "a new strategic relationship that will last long beyond our individual administrations, providing a foundation for peace for the years to come."[17] Indeed, the U.S. withdrawal from the treaty was one of the first indications to Putin that his faith in ongoing strategic partnership as equals was misplaced. Second, Russia was involved in high-level discussions with the United States over the future of the treaty from the earliest stages, avoiding the complaints heard later from Moscow that, instead of consulting beforehand, the United States developed the habit of presenting *faits accomplis*.[18] Finally, this culminated in personal bilateral negotiations at the presidential level: according to Bush, the issues were "discussed with my friend, President Vladimir Putin, over the course of many meetings, many months."[19] This direct engagement at the most senior level — the only one that matters in Russian decisionmaking culture — is also of significance today and will also be referred to later in this monograph.

Subsequently, Bush re-emphasized a strong commitment to missile defense deployment. The missile defense program was reoriented to focus on an integrated, layered defense that would be capable of attacking warheads and missiles in all phases of flight and, eventually, of providing global defenses against missiles of all ranges. As part of this program, the Bush administration started planning for a European missile defense site to intercept ballistic missiles launched from the Middle East.

Poland and Czech Republic — Round One.

Russian alarm at U.S. BMD plans mounted steadily from the mid-2000s[20] as the United States moved closer to implementing a Third Site for missile defense in Europe, eventually intended to comprise a ground-based interceptor (GBI) anti-missile system in Poland and a radar installation in the Czech Republic.

A growing realization of what U.S. renunciation of the ABM Treaty meant in practice led to strenuous and heated Russian opposition to these plans. U.S. efforts to address Russian arguments were not recognized by Moscow as engaging with the fundamental Russian concerns, leading to a spiral of rhetoric from Russian commentators and leaders describing the

Third Site in terms which were barely recognizable to its planners — but that all remain, 6 or more years later, current Russian objections to U.S. BMD plans overall. The themes highlighted in the following text have remained consistent in Russian discourse since 2007, regardless of developments in U.S. plans since then.

Russian Views on the Third Site.[21]

BMD is aimed against no other target than Russia.

> It is already clear that a new phase in the arms race is unfolding in the world. Unfortunately, it does not depend on us, it is not us who are starting it.
>
> *President Putin,*
> *February 8, 2008*

> The problem with possible deployment of ABM elements in Poland and the Czech Republic is that it will not, in our specialists' opinion, have any other goal but monitoring Russia's strategic potential. That is where our harsh response stems from.
>
> *Head of Foreign Ministry*
> *Department for Pan-European*
> *Cooperation, Sergey Ryabkov,*
> *January 23, 2008*

> At the same time, if the third positioning area is created, a radar in the Czech Republic will be monitoring Russian territory up to the Urals and interceptor missiles which are planned to be stationed in Poland will be capable of posing a threat to Russian deterrent arsenal. Therefore, this area — when we are told that it is not aimed at Russia, we should proceed not from intentions, but from facts, real potentials.
>
> *Russian Foreign Minister*
> *Sergey Lavrov,*
> *February 12, 2008*

All this is being done solely in order to deprive Russia of a guaranteed retaliatory strike capability in the event of a nuclear conflict. A guaranteed retaliatory strike has formed the basis of our security strategy since Soviet times, and ensuring this security represents the main and unconditional priority of our military doctrine.

With minimal outlays. the Americans have succeeded not only in ensuring their military presence in Central and Eastern Europe but also in compelling Russia to proceed with its own rearmament at a faster pace than anticipated. Once again, we have been drawn into an arms race via a re-enactment of the scenario of the late-1980s, that brought success for the Americans and constituted one of the reasons for the collapse of the USSR.

Maksim Agarkov, military commentator,
October 22, 2007

The priorities of military threats . . . appear to stem above all from US military policy, particularly the National Security Strategy it is implementing, which represents the chief danger to world and Russian security.

Colonel Vladimir Lutovinov,
Academy of Military Sciences,
June 13, 2007

Dangerous Destabilization.

They decided to deploy defence infrastructure right on our borders. . . . I recall how things went in a similar situation in the mid-1960s. Similar actions by the Soviet Union, when it put missiles in Cuba, precipitated the Cuban Missile Crisis. For us, the technical aspects of the situation are very similar. We have removed the remnants of our bases from Vietnam and dismantled them in Cuba, yet threats of this kind to our own country are today being created right on our borders.

President Putin,
October 26, 2007

We will be forced to take appropriate measures of coun-
teraction. . . . Notice that we are being forced into it. And
the new round of the arms race instigated by the USA
will hardly strengthen the security of the world, including the security of Europe.

Chief of General Staff
Yuriy Baluyevskiy,
July 17, 2007

It is most likely that in the foreseeable future, we will
hear talk about hundreds and even thousands of interceptor missiles in various parts of the world, including
Europe. Poland is just the thin end of the wedge. . . . Just
look at the map and you can see clearly that all this is being done along the perimeter of our borders.

One needs to be very naive to believe that the U.S. missile
defence base in Europe is directed away from Russia.

Russian Foreign Minister
Sergey Lavrov,
February 8, 2008

The initiatives of fresh NATO members, like Poland and
the Czech Republic, to host elements of the global U.S.
missile and air defence system will give the Pentagon a
potential to defeat our strategic nuclear forces. . . . This
means a serious threat to the military [security], and as a
result to the national security of Russia, and could lead to
the disruption of strategic stability in the world.

Colonel-General Boris Cheltsov,
Chief of Staff of the RussianAir Force,
March 14, 2007

Need for Legal Guarantees.

We are forced to take relevant steps which will under no
circumstances allow for the Russian nuclear deterrent
potential to be devalued. . . .

Had the Americans signed a treaty with us under which they would only deploy 10 antimissiles in Poland and one radar in the Czech Republic and would never deploy anything else there, one could agree to that. But they do not sign anything and only make unsubstantiated statements to the effect that they do not threaten us... Russia has already been cheated like that once before.

Strategic Missile Troops (RVSN)
CommanderColonel-General
Nikolay Solovtsov, December 17, 2007

When US Secretary of State Condoleezza Rice and US Defence Secretary Robert Gates were in Moscow [in October 2007], they spoke about a whole range of possible steps on the part of the United States which were proposed as a sort of a guarantee that the US ABM system is not aimed against Russian interests. . . .

We asked to have those 'intentions' in writing, that is in the form of a simple and clear proposal which the USA would be prepared to put forward in practical terms. We waited for almost 6 weeks. That must have been how long it takes inside the US administration to agree a specific wording and, possibly, to hold additional talks with partners. However, what we saw as a result was devoid of those elements.

Deputy Foreign Minister
Sergey Kislyak,
February 5, 2008

Accepting the [Rice-Gates] offer would be like digging our own grave.

Vremya Novostey newspaper,
April 24, 2007

We Will Respond.

A potential threat in this regard does exist for us. And of course, we, as our President and other officials of the Russian Federation have already said more than once, will be forced to take appropriate action to neutralise these threats.

> *Foreign Minister*
> *Sergey Lavrov,*
> *October 15, 2007*

Our General Staff and experts believe that this system threatens our national security, and if it does appear, we will be forced to respond in an appropriate manner. We will then probably be forced to retarget some of our missile systems at these systems, which threaten us. . . . We are warning them in advance that if you take this step, we will be forced to respond in a particular way . . . I believe that I am obliged to say this today directly and honestly, so that later they do not blame themselves for events they themselves will be responsible for.

> *President Putin,*
> *February 14, 2008*

I would like to remind my Polish colleagues of their recent history, which indicates that attempts to situate Poland on the line of confrontation have always led to tragedy. In that way Poland lost nearly one-third of its population during WWII.

> *Russia's representative to NATO,*
> *Dmitry Rogozin,*
> *February 3, 2008*

The responses might be many, and they will all be less expensive than the US actions.

> *Chief of General Staff*
> *Yuriy Baluyevskiy,*
> *May 8, 2007*

Meanwhile, the governments of both Poland and the Czech Republic invested considerable political capital in agreeing to host the U.S. sites in the face of domestic opposition encouraged by vociferous and threatening Russian campaigning. During a tense period immediately following the armed conflict in Georgia in August 2008, then U.S. Secretary of State Condoleezza Rice travelled to Warsaw to sign an agreement on construction of the interceptor site, leading to comment in U.S. media at the time that:

> For many Poles — whose country has been a staunch U.S. ally — the accord represented what they believed would be a guarantee of safety for themselves in the face of a newly assertive Russia.[22]

In July 2009, a group of Central Europe's most recognized former leaders and public figures wrote an open letter to President Barack Obama highlighting missile defense as a symbol of U.S. commitment to Europe and resistance to Russian hostile pressure.[23] Thus when plans for the Third Site BMD installations were cancelled, the immediate reaction was excited relief in Russia and dismay in Central Europe. The announcement of a planned alternative capability was entirely overshadowed by news of the cancellation of the planned radar and GBI site. This was therefore presented by some media as a strategic retreat, or a concession to Russia,[24] which put pressure on relations with both Poland and the Czech Republic.[25] In the case of Poland, an initial sense of betrayal to Russia was heightened by peculiarly insensitive timing; the announcement was made on September 17, 2009, precisely the 70th anniversary of the 1939 invasion of Poland by the Soviet Union.

17

Russia briefly celebrated a perceived victory over the cancellation of plans for installations in Poland and the Czech Republic—and, by implication, the surrender of those countries' interests by the U.S. as a result of Russian pressure.[26] The subsequent realization that cancellation of the Third Site was merely in favor of deployment of different capabilities under the European Phased Adaptive Approach (EPAA) inadvertently reinforced a number of key U.S. messages to Russia: first, announcement of a "cancellation" of an undesirable program is not always good news; second, U.S. plans are subject to radical, sudden and unpredictable change, and not always for the better; and third, as a result, it pays to wait and see before welcoming any new U.S. initiative. These changes fuel Russian distrust in U.S. promises and reinforce Russian arguments that U.S. missile defense capabilities in the future can have very different capabilities than what is currently claimed.

The Current State of EPAA.

Background.

On September 17, 2009, the same day as the Third Site cancellation was made public, President Barack Obama quietly announced a new plan for missile defense, creating the EPAA. The new phased adaptive approach deploys U.S. upper tier sea- and land-based missile defenses in Europe in four phases to supplement NATO lower tier systems as short- and longer-range missile threats from the Middle East proliferate.

The "adaptive" part of the program's title is not an accident, but rather used to show that the missile defense program moving forward will adapt to the ever increasing ballistic missile threat capability but still be able to protect U.S. forces abroad and NATO allies. President Obama stated:

> To put it simply, our new missile defense architecture in Europe will provide stronger, smarter, and swifter defenses of American forces and America's Allies. It is more comprehensive than the previous program; it deploys capabilities that are proven and cost-effective; and it sustains and builds upon our commitment to protect the U.S. homeland against long-range ballistic missile threats; and it ensures and enhances the protection of all our NATO Allies.[27]

This plan calls for the establishment of a fully operational ballistic missile defense system in Europe by 2018, which involved four phases at the time. The first phase consisted of an early warning radar established in Turkey, and BMD-capable *AEGIS* cruisers, complete with the Standard Missile (SM) 3 Block IA medium-range ballistic missile interceptor. U.S. and NATO allies announced initial capability of European missile defense at the May 2012 NATO Summit, much to Russia's chagrin and frustration.

Phase II involves establishment of a land-based SM-3 ballistic missile interceptor site in Romania by 2015, equipped with the more capable SM-3 Block IB able to engage short- and medium-range ballistic missiles. According to Missile Defense Agency's (MDA) Director for International Affairs Nancy Morgan, Phase II broke ground in Romania in September 2013 and will be the first land-based site in Europe. Phase III involves the second and last land-based SM-3 ballistic missile interceptor site in Europe, slated to be operational in Redizkowo, Poland, by 2018, equipped with the SM-3 Block IIA interceptor.

In March 2013, the United States announced the cancellation of EPAA Phase IV, which hinged on introduction of the SM-3 IIB, the technology for which has not yet developed. The SM-3 IIB program was experiencing extended delays, in part due to underfunding and over-ambitious technical aspirations, so the United States decided to place additional interceptors in Fort Greely, Alaska, home of an existing missile defense site in order to protect the U.S. homeland. U.S. Secretary of Defense Chuck Hagel also announced the number of interceptors will increase from 30 to 44.

Hagel also announced plans for extending missile defense plans into Asia, deploying an additional AN/TPY-2 radar in Japan, and called for a possible additional missile defense site in the United States, though he was clear that the decision on deploying the additional site has not been made officially by the Obama administration, but only that studies exploring an additional GBI site would expedite deploying the site, should the decision be made.

Russia's Sectoral Defence Proposal.

Once the planned development phases of EPAA became clear, the Russian objections to BMD resurfaced in full force. The third and fourth stages, intended to counteract longer-range ballistic missiles, were described as a threat to Russian deterrence potential.[28] Meanwhile, the area of coverage of the defensive systems was perceived as threatening to Russia. According to then Russian ambassador to NATO Dmitry Rogozin:

> When the U.S. missile defence map in Europe is drawn for us as an illustration, it turns out that towards the

third and the fourth phases, that is towards 2018 and 2020, the U.S. missile defence sector almost reaches Russia's Urals. This is not what we have agreed on.[29]

Rogozin went on to say that:

> Our partners need to understand that if they want to guarantee their own security, they have their own zone of responsibility. They can do anything they want there, but they should not creep towards us. They should not have the opportunity for their missile defence weapons to shoot down any ballistic targets over our territory, or over third countries.[30]

The solution proposed by Russia was so-called "sectoral defense," or the "sectoral approach," where Russia would ensure protection against missile threats over its own territory, while the United States provided protection for NATO nations. This option, while consistently put forward by Russia as a credible solution that provides for the workable defense of Europe against missiles while addressing Russia's core objections to U.S. plans, was patently unrealistic for several reasons.

- The objection to missiles being shot down by the United States over Russia—"We've already had Chernobyl and that was enough for us"[31]— would seem to rule out the whole basis of the Russian proposal, where Russia shoots down those missiles with the nuclear-based missile defense system currently in place in the Russian Federation.[32]
- Progress in discussing the division of responsibility would never have been possible without much greater Russian transparency over precisely what the Russian Federation could

contribute in terms of future missile defense capability to make its own contribution viable. Despite the pains taken by the United States to explain its plans to the Russian side, including by means of direct briefings, this effort has not at any time been reciprocated in a meaningful manner. This may simply be because Russia does not have the capability to meet its commitments implied in the proposals. According to one informed view, "generally, there is a lack of information and transparency from the Russian side about its missile defense plans (either the Russians don't have plans or they are unwilling to share them)."[33]

• Finally, the basic principle of the sectoral approach — that Russia on the one side and the U.S./NATO nations on the other do not provide missile defense coverage for the other's territory — is unworkable because of simple geographical facts. Russian and NATO territory not only fail to follow neat and straight dividing lines, but in fact overlap thanks to Kaliningrad Oblast sitting on the far side of Latvia and Lithuania from the Russian mainland.

The implication of the last point was that Russia should take missile defense responsibility for some NATO member states. Russia was therefore proposing that NATO should outsource part of its protection to Russia, while at the same time refusing to consider a reciprocal arrangement.[34] The Russian proposal for sectoral missile defense was officially abandoned in mid-July 2011,[35] and yet, it still occasionally reappears in Russian official statements.[36]

Lisbon and Afterwards.

NATO presented its Lisbon Summit in November 2010 as a breakthrough in strategic cooperation between Russia and NATO. In fact, however, this marked the beginning of even greater disappointments for Russia over the progress of BMD provision for Europe. At Lisbon, the United States and NATO agreed to integrate existing NATO member BMD capabilities, with EPAA forming the U.S. contribution.[37] Meanwhile, the concurrent NATO-Russia Council Summit capitalized on the slow stabilization of relations between Russia and NATO after the Georgia war by declaring "a new stage of cooperation towards a true strategic partnership," including exploring cooperation on missile defense.[38]

Moscow remained optimistic during the period immediately following Lisbon for a breakthrough in the United States, or indeed NATO, recognizing and taking into account Russian interests—since this was the Russian understanding of what had been promised at the summit.[39] But this optimism faded rapidly, as Russia saw the United States pushing ahead with plans for EPAA, apparently untroubled by Russian concerns, and with no options for cooperation emerging from the summit. As a result, Russian objections to missile defense plans once again increased in both volume and pitch ahead of a meeting of permanent representatives on the NATO-Russia Council in early July 2011, held in Sochi, Russia, with senior Russian officials, including Foreign Minister Lavrov and Medvedev in attendance.[40] The Sochi meeting was seen in advance as:

a good opportunity to take stock of the implementation of decisions taken in Lisbon—where we are in
contributing to the implementation of a single space
of peace, security and stability in the Euro-Atlantic
area—where we are, what the state of play is, what
should be done.[41]

Predictably enough, assessments of whether or not
this stocktaking was at all productive for BMD discussions varied widely. There was a marked contrast in
the tone of the headlines of reports from the meeting—
from Russian, "NATO and Russia in deadlock over
missile defense,"[42] to German, "Russia warns NATO
over missile defense shield plans,"[43] to independent,
"Russia-NATO Relations Stuck on Missile Defense,"[44]
to NATO's own very distinctive headline—"NATO-
Russia Council makes progress in Sochi."[45] It should
be no surprise that open source reporting on such a
contentious issue as BMD is in effect unrecognizable
between different sources and countries, reinforcing
the need to examine Russian coverage in detail in order to achieve an accurate understanding of both sides
of the conversation.

Thus, by the end of 2011, despite what Russia
had understood as commitments from Lisbon a year
earlier, Moscow saw the United States and NATO
ready to declare Phase I of EPAA operational and on
schedule and hope for any agreement on cooperation
on missile defense receded rapidly.[46] Moscow's disil-
lusionment in negotiations with the United States and
NATO over BMD was made clear in a speech by then-
President Medvedev on November 23, 2011, where
he stated, "We find ourselves facing a *fait accompli.*"[47]
Offers of cooperation by the United States and NATO
were deemed insufficient. For example, according to
NATO Secretary-General Anders Fogh Rasmussen,

NATO had attempted to allay Russian concerns by offering transparency on missile defense programs through exchanges at the NATO-Russia Council and issued "a standing invitation to Russian experts to observe and analyze missile defense tests." Rasmussen wrote that NATO also proposed holding joint NATO-Russian theater missile defense exercises and suggested establishing two joint missile defense centers, one for sharing data and the other for supporting planning.[48] Russia rejected these proposals as insufficient.[49] Nevertheless, NATO officials stated as recently as June 2013 that "these options are still on the table."[50]

"LEGAL GUARANTEES" AND TECHNICAL ARGUMENTS

When the entire history of U.S. BMD plans is reviewed from the Russian perspective, some consistent themes emerge. The history is one of change, inconsistency, and unpredictability, where the United States does not act as a reliable interlocutor. Even when changes are made that appear at first sight to fall in with Russian demands, such as Third Site cancellation, this can mask the development of even more undesirable plans. This sheds light on Russia's discounting of assurances that U.S. BMD plans will not, and are not intended to, challenge Russia's deterrent potential and Russia's consequent repeated demands for "legally binding guarantees" that this is the case.

There is no shortage of statements on record by both U.S. and NATO officials that Russia is not the target of European BMD plans and that the intention is not to undermine strategic stability.[51] Unfortunately, saying so does not make it so in Russian eyes. Washington and NATO have offered political guarantees of

good faith to Moscow during several rounds of negotiations, but history has shown Moscow that with every U.S. presidential administration, the focus, goals,
and momentum of the U.S. missile defense system
change. In this light, it becomes less of a surprise that
Moscow gives little weight to U.S. assurances over
BMD—since it sees the United States doing the same.
Russia therefore asks for a more binding commitment
from the United States.

Speaking in 2011, Russian Foreign Minister Sergey
Lavrov explained this as follows:

> We propose agreeing on guarantees that the future
> [EPAA] system will not be aimed against Russia. . . .
> we propose agreeing on criteria to verify in practice
> that the stated purpose of the project—namely, to
> ward off missile threats from outside the Euro-Atlan-
> tic region—will actually be observed. The Americans
> are not yet ready for that; they give assurances that
> there are no plans to aim this system against Russia.
> But they refer to the fact that the Senate has forbade
> the administration to limit the future development
> of missile defence in any way—in other words, there
> may be a fifth, sixth, seventh, etc. phase, which also
> does not add much to predictability.
>
> Our position is simple: if you say that the system is not
> aimed against Russia, why not put it on paper?[52]

The U.S. refusal (and indeed political inability) to
give binding commitments on limitations to the capability of BMD systems is accompanied by a wealth
of expert opinion pointing out that the "legal guarantees" would be inappropriate and unworkable. Sam-
uel Charap of the International Institute of Strategic
Studies (IISS) notes that the United States is, in effect,
being called on to give guarantees that Russia should

be allowed to annihilate it at will,[53] while leading disarmament and arms control specialist Paul Schulte notes the probable ineffectiveness of legal agreements constraining "a state interested in the thermo-nuclear incineration of millions of your citizens."[54] Informed commentary within Russia also notes difficulties with the demand. According to Aleksey Arbatov, leading commentator and head of the Centre for International Security of the Institute for International Economy and International Relations of the Russian Academy of Sciences, "Russia is demanding some sort of legal guarantees, but is not saying exactly what type of guarantees. If Russia wants a new treaty limiting missile defence, the USA and NATO will not do it." Furthermore, Arbatov writes, the guarantees are entirely one-sided: Russia has no intention of giving anyone any guarantees regarding its own planned air and space defence system; "on the contrary, we openly say that this system is aimed against the USA and NATO."[55] As noted by Aleksandr Stukalin in the respected *Moscow Defense Brief* quarterly:

> the notion of unilateral 'legally binding guarantees' seems to be a curious new invention by the Russian negotiators, since there are no historical precedents of such guarantees . . . how exactly are the 'guarantees' demanded by Russia supposed to work?[56]

The impossibility for the U.S. side of subscribing to any restriction on missile defense plans that would require Senate ratification[57] is an obstacle fully recognized and understood by Russia. Finally, even legal guarantees are suspect—treaty obligations, like those contained in the ABM Treaty, can be, and indeed have been, renounced. But the fact that Russia's demands are unworkable does nothing to reduce the "intensity and repetitiveness" of Russian insistence on its understanding of international law and on the necessity for "legally-binding agreements."[58] This is entirely consistent with calls for treaty arrangements in other and broader areas of concern to Moscow, such as the persistent Russian push for a new "European Security Treaty," and it should be expected to remain an underlying theme of Russian demands in future.

Technical Issues.

Russia's objections to U.S. missile defense systems in Europe hinge on the assumption that, at some future stage in their development, they will be capable of reducing the effectiveness of strategic missiles launched from Russia. The technological capabilities of currently deployed systems are less alarming than what was promised for the future under Phases III and IV of EPAA, and it is against threatening future developments that Russia has consistently sought protective guarantees.

Independent critics claim BMD technologies overall remain mostly unproven to date, often run behind schedule, have significant cost overruns, and would have limited ability to defend against an actual ballistic missile attack.[59] But Russian officials note that once any technology is fielded, the United States can decide at any time to increase the number of deployed interceptors or modify existing equipment with more advanced software and hardware.

Despite the unified and dogmatic position officially presented by Russia that EPAA poses a threat to Russian deterrence, technical debates do take place in Russia between responsible and informed individuals, arriving at a range of different conclusions about the real implications for Russia of missile defense plans.[60] Highly qualified Russian experts do disagree with the official Russian line. Colonel-General (Retired) Viktor Yesin, formerly Chief of Staff of Russia's Strategic Missile Forces, does so regularly in Russian sources, including in those media that would normally imply official blessing.[61] Similarly, Major-General (Retired) Vladimir Dvorkin, also formerly of the Russian Strategic Missile Forces and credited with significant contributions to formulating Soviet and Russian positions at strategic arms control negotiations, consistently puts forward reasoned arguments that cast doubt on Russian official claims for the efficacy and intended target of EPAA.[62] According to Yury Solomonov, chief designer of the Moscow Institute of Thermal Technology (Russia's premier strategic missile design bureau), "In most cases—and I'm saying this absolutely officially and taking responsibility—the threat to our strategic potential has simply been invented."[63]

Knowledgeable individuals from both the United States and Russia have put forward technical arguments outlining precisely at which point U.S. missiles would, in theory, be capable of intercepting Russian ICBMs. As might be expected, given that the arguments rest on commonly accepted laws of physics, there is a degree of congruence between independent assessments from Russia and from the United States. For example, the conclusions reached by Yesin, cited earlier, with Major-General Yevgeniy Savostyanov in April 2012[64] are broadly similar to those of Yousaf Butt and Theodore Postol in a Federation of American Scientists report in September 2011.[65] Both agree that, on a purely technical basis, U.S. BMD plans pose little or no threat to Russia's nuclear deterrent capability—especially given the location of fixed Russian missile bases and the Russian ability to use countermeasures—and this assessment has only been strengthened by the cancellation of the SM3 Block IIB missile, whose likely capabilities were used for the worst case assessments.

On this basis, it could reasonably be hoped that Russia and the United States could reach baseline agreements on the precise point in BMD technology development at which Russia has legitimate cause for concern—especially given repeated bilateral expert consultations, including at the Moscow conference on missile defense in May 2012.[66] But even if technical discussion behind closed doors can reach agreement on immutable physical realities, Russia apparently does not find this possible in public debate, even at those presentations where Russia is seeking through graphics and modeling to demonstrate the exact impact of BMD on Russian deterrence. At one such demonstration held at the Russian Embassy in London in June 2012, the technical assumptions behind the modeled successful intercepts of Russian missiles were questioned from the audience; rather than defending or explaining the simulation, the Russian response was simply that the "probability of interception depends on factors we will not discuss here."[67] Similarly, when asked to reconcile Russia's official position with the views of acknowledged Russian subject matter experts such as Dvorkin, Russia's Deputy Head of Mission to NATO was brusque:

> There are a lot of experts expressing their personal views on things. Every expert has the right to express his own views. . . . That is an opinion of a man [Dvorkin] who as far as I know retired some time ago.[68]

This failure to engage with challenges to Russian statements strongly reinforces the view that the Russian objections to BMD are, in fact, insubstantial and have no basis in any realistic technical capability to challenge Russian deterrence. However, the majority of the experts cited earlier also agreed that strict technical capabilities are not the only criterion for determining whether the planned EPAA Phase IV was destabilizing and a threat to Russia, and a range of political, historical, and other factors are in play. This became abundantly clear when Phase IV was cancelled in March 2013.

EPAA PHASE IV CANCELLED

There was widespread expectation in the United States and its allies that the decision to cancel EPAA Phase IV would be welcomed with appreciation by Russia, as at first sight this removed many of the Russian objections to the planned development of EPAA. As put by Yesin, "The decision not to place SM-3 missiles with increased combat capabilities [Block IIB] in Europe . . . will eliminate the main irritant for Russia."[69] Instead, the initial reaction from Moscow was a studied silence.

Following the 2009 experience of Third Site cancellation, Russia no doubt wished to avoid premature expressions of enthusiasm. But there were other, more significant reasons for the subdued response. In private discussions, Russian officials noted that the reaction to cancellation of EPAA Phase 4 was skeptical because of the overall situation and broader context in which it was made: the stated reasons for the cancellation were nothing to do with Russia, the decision was presented by the United States as the program being "restructured" on technical grounds, rather than cancelled, giving no guarantee that it would not return at a later date; and crucially, the development suggested that other future changes of plan and direction are likely.[70]

As noted earlier, "adaptive" is a key word in the title of the EPAA program. But according to First Secretary of Russia's Mission to NATO Sergei Malyugin, speaking at the 2013 Royal United Services Institute (RUSI) Missile Defence Conference, "The adaptive approach is a little *too* adaptive." What from the U.S. side looks like flexibility to develop in accordance with an evolving threat seems inconsistent, unpredictable, and therefore destabilizing to Russia. Changes like these do not instill confidence in U.S. assurances and lend weight to Russia's perceived need for legally binding guarantees, such as a formal treaty. Thus while the eventual Russian response to Hagel's announcement was "cautiously optimistic," it was also careful to state that while the move is appreciated, the cancellation does not change Russian concerns that European BMD systems may eventually target Russia.[71]

What the U.S. cancellation of phase IV has seemed to accelerate was Russian interest in returning to negotiations with the United States over missile defense in Europe. Only now, Russia no longer views missile defense as only a European security issue – now Russia views missile defense as worldwide and is increasingly concerned about U.S. expansion – primarily U.S. missile defense sites surrounding Russia from both the East and West. In the same vein, Moscow increasingly relays to Washington that Moscow is growing less interested in bilateral missile defense talks and wants to include other nations with missile defense interests into the fold of discussions – namely China. This will undoubtedly make future missile defense discussions difficult for U.S. policymakers.[72]

This issue appears closely aligned with the U.S. "pivot" to the East and how Russia is accounting for that pivot in its own security calculus, including potentially becoming more involved in Asia and aligning more closely with China on missile defense. It is at present unclear to what extent Russia recognizes that the need for missile defense capability is more pressing in Northeast Asia than in Europe,[73] but Asia features much less prominently in Moscow's anti-BMD campaign, arguably in part because Russian influence on and interest in countries threatened by North Korean weapons is much less than in Central Europe.

A further complicating factor for future negotiation is the Russian desire to fold missile defense dialogue into all areas of arms control discussion, including on conventional arms control in Europe and further nuclear reductions. According to Nikolai Korchunov:

> Missile defence is only one element of security which is more and more intertwined, and is being influenced by a number of inter-related and interconnected factors. It is really difficult to analyse security only from the stand-point of missile defence without taking into account conventional arms, the Prompt Global Strike concept and the threat of the weaponisation of outer space. The failure to reach a compromise on missile defence could also complicate the future prospects of the disarmament process.[74]

Thus the missile defense issue is being raised in response to a number of different topics, including the proposal to Russia by the Obama administration for negotiations on both conventional weapons control and further reductions in nuclear arms beyond New Strategic Arms Reduction Treaty (START).[75] The result, according to one senior British official, is "strategic constipation," as the interlinking of all issues makes it impossible to resolve any single one.

RUSSIA – OTHER FACTORS

As noted earlier, the pure technical capabilities of U.S. missile defense systems are not the only means by which they pose a challenge to Russia. There are a number of other historical and geopolitical considerations affecting Russian decisionmaking on BMD that may not be intuitively obvious when the issue is viewed from a U.S. perspective.

Self-Perception and Geopolitical Perspective.

Russian objections to BMD plans refer consistently to threats to strategic stability. The shared understanding of this term as applied to deterrence during the Cold War is no longer in force: to Western policymakers, it now has entirely different implications, whereas in Russia, as with so much else, the definition of the term has not moved on—leading to yet more misunderstanding in bilateral discussion.[76]

One implication of this is that defensive systems that could theoretically counter even a small part of Russia's nuclear deterrence potential have strategic implications for Russia out of all proportion to their actual degrading effect. As Paul Schulte notes in a 2013 paper, whether or not Russia's deterrence can, in fact, be neutralized by BMD, the fact that it is undermined and called into question is in itself destabilizing.[77]

Allied to this is the Russian perception of nuclear weapons as a guarantee, and indeed a symbol, of national status. In the first decade after the end of the

Soviet Union, the old quip comparing the country with "Upper Volta with nuclear weapons" resurfaced regularly among Russia-watchers.[78] If nuclear weapons were all that stood between Russia and Third World status, the implications of taking the weapons away were clear enough. Regardless that Russia today is a very different country from that of the 1990s, the status of nuclear weapons in the national psyche remains the same. According to former U.S. diplomat Wayne Merry:

> Anything like BMD which contains the potential — or even the perception of the potential — to compromise the integrity or stature of the Russian nuclear arsenal is seen by policymakers in Moscow as a danger not only to the country's security but to its historic identity as a great state.[79]

This contrasts with the approach taken in the United States and other states, which would happily renounce nuclear weapons altogether were such a thing possible. Merry continues:

> If all nuclear weapons were by magic to disappear from the earth overnight, American security would be enhanced due to our dominance in non-nuclear military technologies and forces; by contrast, Russia would face a fundamental crisis of national identity. . . . Thus, American talk of global "nuclear zero" is viewed in Moscow as inspired by the goal of U.S. non-nuclear hegemony, rather than to free the world from nuclear fear.[80]

Another related issue is the inalienable Russian perception that Russia matters in everything and is constantly at the forefront of U.S. policymakers' minds. While Rogozin may state that "European missile defence . . . can be created only with Russia's participation. Without Russia, there will be no missile defence,"[81] this is hard to reconcile with the progress of missile defense plans—without Russian participation—to date. In fact, Russia has very few levers with which to influence U.S. decisionmaking. Nevertheless, the Russian urge to maintain a self-perceived superpower status, despite all economic, technical, and military evidence to the contrary, leads it to seek to use political constraints on the United States to compensate for its long-term relative decline. In essence, diplomatic power is the only lever that Russia retains to project power beyond its immediate neighbors.

Meanwhile, Russia believes that it can manage through political relations those countries that the United States perceives as a potential missile threat, including Iran. Furthermore, Russia does not share the U.S. threat perception; it does not believe Iran has the intent, nor the capability, to engage the United States with ballistic missiles.

Moscow questions U.S. published assessments of Iranian missile technology but also points out that since the United States clearly will not allow Iran to develop a nuclear capability, it cannot logically be concerned about a nuclear threat to Europe from Iran. Therefore, the political effort and capital going into EPAA must be designed for a more established missile threat: Russia.

But even if Russia were to accept that a threat from Iran exists, it is reluctant to legitimize U.S. efforts to counter it today because of concerns—validated by recent U.S. statements and actions—over how the countermeasures will develop in the medium to long term. In addition, domestic Russian politics need to be considered. The current Russian leadership would find it challenging to emphasize the peaceable nature of U.S. BMD plans after so much effort has been expended on portraying them as an existential threat to Russia. A precedent for this challenge exists: Russian approval of Ulyanovsk as a site for a transit hub on the Northern Distribution Network to facilitate U.S., NATO, and allied drawdown from Afghanistan caused a severe domestic political backlash after years of the Russian public absorbing largely hostile messaging about NATO.[82]

One additional factor that is particularly unhelpful in this context is the internal tension within the United States, between the desire to present BMD as a credible system that will, in fact, deter its target audience, and playing down its current and potential capabilities in order not to lend substance to Russian objections. The balance is not always well maintained: at the same time Russia was being assured publicly that ground-based interceptors to be sited in Poland could not possibly challenge the Russian nuclear deterrent because of their very limited number, statements were also being made that "We will be able to put hundreds of interceptors in the air at a given time . . . within the next several years."[83]

As put by Brigadier-General Lauri Kiianlinna, "like beauty, a credible defence posture is in the eye of the beholder."[84] It remains the case that both adversaries and unrelated third parties, including Russia, may have more faith in the deterrent potential of missile defense than its creators in the United States. Russia's military doctrine emphasizes the threat of hostile military infrastructure "approaching Russia's borders," and it is easy, if desired, to read planned installations in Poland and Romania, and Aegis BMD capabilities afloat off the Russian coastline, as a case in point.[85]

The perception is stronger in Russian minds than in Western ones that missile defense is a reversal of the post-Cold-War processes of the last 20 years: instead of disarming, withdrawing, and closing down, this is an introduction of new capabilities. This is why Russia points to a reversal of a security trend and a shift in strategic balance.[86] This exacerbates the Russian perception of the United States as an irresponsible actor that has not learned strategic lessons from intervention in Afghanistan, Iraq, and Libya, and may in the future be tempted to meddle in Russia. EPAA, and expanded BMD capabilities in the Pacific, give rise to a Russian sensation of encirclement by U.S. interceptor missiles and U.S.-sponsored forces in Europe, the Middle East, and the Asia Pacific. In fact, a slide repeatedly shown by Morgan showing global missile defense deployments is eerily reminiscent of Soviet propaganda images from the Cold War, showing Russia surrounded on all sides and across the Arctic by missiles and troops fielded by the United States and its imperialist proxies.

Economic Issues.

The suggestion that Russia's strategic response to SDI in the 1980s hastened the demise of the Soviet Union has already been discussed. Thirty years later, just as in the case of discussion of technical capabilities, informed Russian experts are perfectly prepared to voice opinions that do not fall in with official policy, warning of similar consequences that might ensue for Russia from heavy investment in countermeasures to defeat U.S. BMD plans:

In principle, Russia is capable of taking these steps, but it must consider the economic and political price of doing so. This would mean huge spending on a new arms race. In the case of the hypotonic Russian economy, this is akin to a person with acute anaemia donating blood. It is unlikely that we could cope with this in the long run.[87]

This consideration is given extra weight by the perception with hindsight that the Soviet response to SDI was entirely unnecessary because SDI's technological basis was, in fact, illusory. As put by Solomonov, speaking directly to Putin in February 2012, "[SDI] tied up huge intellectual, material and financial resources. . . . it was a complete fraud." Speaking at the same round table with Putin, Sergey Rogov, Director of the Russian Academy of Sciences' Institute for U.S. and Canadian Studies, continued that:

We are repeating the mistakes of 29 years ago. When Reagan came up with "Star Wars," some people in our country decided that that was it, it was the end of the world. . . . But now, in my opinion, there is a real opportunity to avoid past mistakes.[88]

Russia thus finds itself faced with a choice of existential threats: the U.S. BMD plans have the theoretical potential either to devalue Russia's nuclear deterrent, its last-ditch guarantee of statehood and protection of its interests, or to draw Russia into an arms race whose previous iteration contributed to the downfall of the state in which the current generation of Russian leaders were born and raised — with all the dire consequences they observed at first-hand in the 1990s.

Russia's Proposed Responses.

Current Russian statements carry yet another echo of past debates, only with the roles of the United States and USSR reversed: when told that it is inconceivable that the United States would consider a nuclear attack on Russia, the Russian response is the same as that of the United States during the Cold War—that a nation cannot gamble its security on another state's stated intentions, but only on its developing capabilities.[89] To Western ears, this sounds like Cold-War era thinking; but it needs to be placed in the context of Russia's perception of being both encircled and threatened by the capability gap between the United States and Russia—perceptions that helped shape Soviet Cold War thinking. This in turn provides context for the hostility of Russian statements and outright threats over missile defense.

One of the most significant considerations informing Russian attitudes to BMD is the dramatic gap that remains between Russian and U.S. military capability. Russia's perception of strategic vulnerability has led to an emphasis on aerospace defense and strategic offensive weapons in the ongoing program of military transformation and re-investment in defense in an attempt to close the gap—in spite of the warnings over the consequences for Russia of a new arms race, and a plethora of expert analysis observing that the real military threat to Russia is an entirely different one.[90] The detailed status and goals of the transformation effort lie outside the scope of this monograph,[91] but some of the most recent adjustments at the time of this writing place even greater weight on strategic weapons systems and relegate the ground forces still further in the queue for funding.[92] As put by Putin:

We must take into account the realities of the day, we cannot allow the strategic deterrence system to be upset or the effectiveness of our nuclear forces to be decreased. For this reason the creation of the aerospace defense system will continue to be one of the key priorities in military development.[93]

The new aerospace defense command (*Voyenno-kosmicheskaya oborona* or VKO) is being prioritized for funding not only in response to the nuclear threat, but also to a perception of vulnerability to U.S. conventional precision strike capabilities. Also, according to Putin in June 2013, following the Presidential Summit on the sidelines of the G8 Summit in the UK:

We see that work is active around the world on developing high-precision conventional weapons systems that in their strike capabilities come close to strategic nuclear weapons. Countries that have such weapons substantially increase their offensive capability.[94]

But Russian reporting also suggests prioritization of countermeasures specifically intended to overcome U.S. BMD capabilities. According to Russian researcher Dr. Igor Sutyagin, Russia is investing heavily in a range of means of both counteracting and defeating U.S. BMD systems, which are "based on mature Soviet technology, just updating the electronics by two generations." These include penetration aids; advanced decoys; maneuverable and gliding re-entry vehicles (RVs); concealment measures for RVs; means for blinding infrared and radar seekers; nuclear force protection measures, including road and rail mobile ICBMs; seabed laid ballistic missile systems; and multilayered missile defense systems for Russia's own fixed installations.[95] As in other fields, Russian actions and statements now mirror those of the United States in previous decades, in this case with the U.S. response to the Moscow ABM site: it was reported to the House Armed Services Committee in 1987 that the Soviet ABM system could be penetrated by ICBMs equipped with highly effective chaff and decoys, and furthermore that "if the Soviets should deploy more advanced or proliferated defenses we have new penetration aids as counters."[96]

As part of the response to EPAA, Russia's engagement with the new START has repeatedly been questioned. According to Rogozin, "At a certain stage a situation could arise when we will have to leave the START-3 treaty."[97] There is skepticism as to how realistic this threat may be. It had already been threatened before the Sochi summit in 2011 that failure to fall in with Russian requests for sectoral defense could lead to Russia withdrawing from START[98]—a stipulation that was then quietly dropped.

Official Russian statements send mixed messages on where, and when, precisely Russia's red lines lie. On the one hand, Lavrov states that there are no deadlines for agreement,[99] and Rogozin confirms that "in general, we do not use the language of ultimatums. One should learn to talk to the West with dignity and from a position of confidence in our own powers."[100] On the other, there are plentiful statements and comments hinting at the unfortunate consequences of failure to reach an agreement satisfactory to Russia. In 2011, for example, Korchunov suggested:

> I think in the case when we disagree and Russian concerns are not assuaged it could have unfortunate consequences for European security. These things should

be regarded and perceived in a much broader context of our relationship with the US—the interrelationship between offensive and defensive arms is spelled out in the Russia-US START Treaty. Of course if such an unfortunate scenario develops it will force us to take measures. The logic is simple and clear: if one side increases anti-ballistic capabilities it forces the other side to build up its offensive arms.[101]

Finally, Russia has repeatedly threatened as a last resort to take direct military action against U.S. facilities if its concerns are not heeded. As expressed in one commentary in July 2011, if no legal guarantee is received from the United States, Russia:

will deploy our missile grouping on the Western borders and aim our missiles at the European missile defence installations. . . . That will be the answer in any case if they try to deprive us of the dearest thing that any Russian has, our nuclear shield.[102]

The same threat has been repeated on numerous occasions by Putin and Medvedev: as put by Medvedev in November 2011, Russia may "deploy modern offensive weapon systems in the west and south of the country, ensuring our ability to take out any part of the US missile defence system in Europe."[103]

OUTLOOK AND POLICY IMPLICATIONS

The recent history of the missile defense conversation with Russia has been one of repeated and unsuccessful attempts by the United States and NATO to find an accommodation to allay Russian concerns. A variety of approaches have been attempted in order to convince Moscow that EPAA—as well as the larger concept of BMD overall—is not designed against or intended to target Russia, nor its strategic deterrent. Several initiatives were under way in 2012 alone, including a joint missile defense exercise in Germany, and a report by the multinational Euro-Atlantic Security Initiative group.[104] Yet none of these attempts have mitigated Russia's trenchant opposition to the U.S. plans.

The ineluctable block to progress in discussions of BMD between the United States and Russia is that the two nations' fundamental interests simply do not align, and there is, therefore, no overlap at all between the desired end states of each side. The United States sees BMD capability as an essential means of protection for the United States and its allies; Russia sees the exact reverse, and requires an absence of BMD systems from Europe to ensure its own security. There is simply no room for compromise between these two polar opposites. The best that U.S. policymakers can do, therefore, is engage with the Russian fears in open dialogue, in a continued attempt to assuage Russian concerns and thereby avoid a political miscalculation that could ultimately lead to a real military problem.

In the meantime, the United States should also consider the messaging that is directed at its European allies, as well as at Russia. It was widely recognized that the 2013 news of cancellation of EPAA Phase IV, while still unwelcome for Europe, was delivered in a greatly more competent manner than the 2009 announcement of cancellation of earlier plans for installations in Poland and the Czech Republic. Yet, private diplomatic work with allied governments does not always translate into European media treatment, or public opinion, or expert commentary that is sympathetic to U.S. changes of plan. Even independent experts from third countries may agree that the current U.S. BMD plans are no challenge to Russia's deterrent, but at the same time remain highly critical of the handling of EPAA and its effects on U.S. allies. According to Stefan Forss, "The U.S. did its allies a big disservice putting so much political weight into SM-3 IIB. The Poles and others feel betrayed. . . . Politics should be based on facts, not technical illusions."[105]

The experience of 2009 showed the importance of public opinion in Central Europe and the amount of political capital that allies potentially have to expend in order to be able to support U.S. plans. In this area, the United States would benefit from enhanced efforts to convince European publics that changes of plan over EPAA do not mean a reduced commitment by the United States to European security. As put by the Center for European Policy Analysis, a U.S. think tank:

[The U.S.] Administration must now deal with the very real fear among Europeans that last week's EPAA cancellation was just the first in a series of "salami slices" that, deliberately or not, will ultimately result in the eventual, *de facto* death of the U.S. missile defense program in Europe. Rightly or wrongly, this has been the suspicion of many Polish and American observers since the onset of the Administration's planning for EPAA. . . . [By] removing the one component of America's BMD program in Europe that is directly relevant to the defense of the continental United States, the cancellation is likely to create an irresistible opening for voices on Capitol Hill to argue against the program entirely. Under this logic, a system that only defends Europe should no longer be America's financial responsibility. Some allies are not irrational in their growing, if politely muted, suspicion that greater "flexibility" on BMD could indeed eventually enter into the cards in strategic nuclear talks with Moscow.[106]

Perception of U.S. commitment to Europe becomes an even more acute issue in the light of U.S. statements on a "pivot" to Asia. The subsequent rebranding of the "pivot" to a "rebalancing," among a number of other soothing synonyms adopted by the U.S. leadership, does little to address concerns over a possible reduction of the relative weight of the United States in European security[107] — which is, after all, a long-standing Russian aim.[108]

The hostile messaging emanating from Russia is an undeniable factor in Central European public opinion. But at the political level, working with Russia as a dialogue partner in large part consists of the art of filtering out angry noises and bluster in order to determine where the real concerns, red lines, and threats of consequences actually lie. At the same time, just because a Russian threat of direct military action in Europe seems inconceivable to us does not mean that it should be ruled out. Russian perception of military action as a valid foreign policy tool was reinforced by the results of the armed conflict in Georgia in 2008. Although widely portrayed in foreign media and analysis as self-defeating, and despite the fact that it highlighted severe deficiencies in Russian military capability, the conflict with Georgia, in fact, resolved a number of key doctrinal challenges for Russia and demonstrated that when Russia says often and loud enough that it will do something, something does occasionally happen.[109] It should be recalled that just as in 2008, Russia would weigh the advantages and disadvantages of direct military intervention abroad to protect its perceived security interests by very different criteria than would the United States.[110]

One of the Russian responses to EPAA that has attracted the most attention overseas has been the threat of deploying Russia's own offensive missile systems, specifically SS-26 Iskander missiles, to the Kaliningrad Region, thereby greatly extending their reach into NATO territory.[111] But it is misleading to link this promise solely to EPAA. The threat of forward deployment of Iskanders has been a staple of Russian rhetoric since long before 2009 and is reliably wheeled out in many other cases when Russia feels it needs to make a point because its interests are being neglected — for example, ahead of the accession to NATO of Estonia, Latvia, and Lithuania in 2004. Previous instances even pre-date the availability of Iskander systems; analogous threats of forward deployment of the Tochka-U system date back at least to 2001.

Throughout this period, Russia has seen that its attention-seeking behavior has been richly rewarded by strong reactions from European media and from those policymaking establishments in partner countries that have failed to retain the institutional memory to realize that the threat cannot in any way be described as a new development. This confirms for Russia that repeated threats of deployments of advanced systems to Kaliningrad are profitable and worthwhile, and they should be expected to continue for as long as they provoke the desired response. Nevertheless, as with the case of deployment of S-400 Triumf systems to Kaliningrad, which was similarly preceded by a lengthy series of threatening statements, they should also be considered as indicative of a long-term rollout plan by the Russian armed forces that eventually will be implemented anyway.[112]

The United States can therefore expect Russia to deploy weapons systems to counter U.S. missile defense, but the timing of this deployment, and the systems used, will most probably depend on the progress of implementation of EPAA. Key dates in this respect are the beginning of construction at the Romanian site in September 2013 and at the Polish site in 2018. In addition, given the history of U.S. changes of plan linked to changes in presidential administration, Russia may be less inclined to seek a conclusive resolution before the next U.S. presidential election in 2016.

Russia is faced with a choice between an early agreement with the current U.S. President, that they hope will be honored by the next incumbent, or the much more realistic prospect of waiting for the 2016-18 window between the next U.S. election and the beginning of construction at the Polish site. Ahead of this time, Russia can wait to see what is offered by the United States and then cherry-pick its preferred option; but after the start of construction in Poland, Russia loses political leverage, reducing the number of alternative courses of action available by Russia other than a purely military response. In this period, Russia could either accept U.S. or NATO offers of transparency and cooperation or make its own counteroffer of cooperation in an area that is important to the United States.

As noted previously, Russian withdrawal from the START appears unlikely. It is also questionable whether renewed discussion by Russia of withdrawal from the Intermediate Nuclear Forces (INF) Treaty would lead to action, given the extent to which the treaty serves Russian interests by restraining an area of U.S. conventional superiority.[113] The Russian demands for "legally binding guarantees," up to and including a new treaty agreement, should be expected to continue. But despite the lack of realism of the current phrasing of the Russian demands, another underlying factor that provides the United States with leverage is the validation a bilateral treaty with the United States would provide for Russia's self-perception as a great power and the nominal equal of the United States. The prospect of a treaty arrangement that recognizes the special role of the Russian Federation may well provide a meaningful incentive in further discussions with Moscow, regardless of the actual eventual content of any agreement reached.

Take It To The Top.

In an unscripted moment picked up by news cameras on March 26, 2012, President Obama told outgoing Russian President Medvedev that there is a better chance of dealing with the sensitive issue of missile defense after the U.S. presidential elections the following November. "This is my last election," Obama said. "After my election, I have more flexibility." As noted previously with the example of U.S. withdrawal from the ABM Treaty, this direct leader engagement on a personal level carries weight in discussions with Russia.

Discussions on missile defense between Lavrov and Rasmussen in April 2013 decided publicly to "leave such a fundamental issue to the Presidents of the Russian Federation and the United States."[114] Accordingly, the most recent initiative at the time of this writing is a round of negotiations directly between Obama and Putin, commencing with a letter from Obama to Putin suggesting another way forward on missile defense cooperation focused on transparency between the United States and Russia on BMD technical capabilities.[115] If any agreement at all can be reached with Russia on BMD, it is likely to be through this bilateral presidential route; in any case, on the Russian side, progress on a decision of this magnitude could not be made without authorization from the very highest level. According to Foreign Minister Lavrov, speaking ahead of the 2011 Sochi summit:

> The subject of missile defence for obvious reasons can hardly be tackled by the ambassadors. Deliberation on it proceeds at the summit and high levels. There are special arrangements, especially between Russia and the United States.[116]

These "special arrangements" at present constitute the only visible prospect for a resolution with Russia before the next U.S. election cycle.

CONCLUSION

Viewed from Moscow, the history of U.S. BMD development is one of inconsistency, unpredictability, and doubtful assurances. Russia can have little confidence that this pattern will not continue. As put by one NATO official, "US plans have changed twice in 4 years, and there are still 5 years to go till 2018."[117]

According to a Russian official who requested anonymity, Russia's key problem with EPAA is that the United States says it is "a limited capability against a limited threat, but then will not accept any limitations on this so-called limited capability."[118] Indeed, at the RUSI Missile Defence Conference in London, United Kingdom (UK), in June 2013, Deputy Assistant Secretary of State Frank Rose felt the need to repeat three times that the United States "cannot and will not" accept limitations on the capabilities of BMD systems.

Thus, uncertainty over U.S. planning combines with uncertainty over the ultimate technological capabilities of BMD systems to introduce a fundamental element of unpredictability to Russia's assessments of its own security. A primary Russian concern, as repeatedly emphasized in the most recent iteration of its Foreign Policy Concept, is the maintenance of "stability";[119] U.S. missile defense plans mount a direct challenge to this aim.

Finally, any assessment of Russia's future responses to further BMD developments must take into account the very different Russian perception of two key issues: first, the role nuclear weapons play for the state; and second, the role Russia plays in the world. As put by Wayne Merry:

> Ultimately, for Russia the issue is not Iran, nor NATO, nor the US, nor specific systems. American progress toward balancing ballistic missiles with credible defenses erodes the *status quo* essential to Moscow's assertion of great power status. Far from seeing nuclear weapons as a necessary evil of the modern world, Russia's elites perceive them as the bedrock of its state power and global identity for the foreseeable future. That is the starting point for any U.S. dialogue, let alone negotiation, with Russia on BMD.[120]

ENDNOTES

1. "Statement by the Press Secretary on the President's Travel to Russia," Washington, DC: White House Office of the Press Secretary, August 7, 2013, available from *www.whitehouse.gov/the-press-office/2013/08/07/statement-press-secretary-president-s-travel-russia*.

2. As noted in exasperated tone by Ambassador Alexander Vershbow in June 2013, "Every time we remove a perceived hurdle, the Russians erect another."

3. "Europe Diary: Missile Defence," BBC News, June 1, 2007, available from *news.bbc.co.uk/1/hi/world/europe/6704669.stm*.

4. Dmitry Medvedev, "Statement in connection with the situation concerning the NATO countries' missile defence system in Europe," Russian presidential website, November 23, 2011, available from *eng.kremlin.ru/news/3115*.

5. "Missile Defense: The First 60 Years," Missile Defense Agency (MDA).

6. MDA website: *www.mda.mil/news/history_resources.html*.

7. "Treaty on the Limitation of Anti-Ballistic Missile Systems (ABM Treaty)," Nuclear Threat Initiative, available from *www.nti.org/treaties-and-regimes/treaty-limitation-anti-ballistic-missile-systems-abm-treaty/*.

8. "Backgrounder: U.S. Ballistic Missile Defense," Washington, DC: Council on Foreign Relations, available from *www.cfr.org/missile-defense/us-ballistic-missile-defense/p30607*.

9. Email exchange with author, July 2013.

10. "Safeguard," Washington, DC: Federation of American Scientists, available from *www.fas.org/spp/starwars/program/safeguard.htm*. See also "Sprint," *Nuclear ABMS of the USA*, available from *www.nuclearabms.info/Sprint.html*.

11. This remains the case despite doubts over the Soviet system's capability. See "History of Russia's ABM System," Cambridge, MA: Union of Concerned Scientists, available from *www.ucsusa.org/nuclear_weapons_and_global_security/missile_defense/policy_issues/history-of-russias.html*.

12. For video of the speech, see "Reagan Announces SDI," PBS Video, available from *video.pbs.org/video/1781119310/*.

13. Andropov interview in *Pravda*, March 26, 1983, quoted in *Reuters*, "Excerpts From The Interview With Andropov," March 27, 1983.

14. In 1993, the Strategic Defense Initiative Organization was renamed the Ballistic Missile Defense Organization. Then-Secretary of Defense Les Aspin "gave credit to SDI for helping to end the Cold War." See MDA website, available from *www.mda.mil/ news/history_resources.html*.

15. Vladimir Putin, *"Poslaniye Federalnomu Sobraniyu Rossiyskoy Federatsii"* ("Address to the Federal Assembly of the Russian Federation"), May 10, 2006, available from *archive.kremlin.ru/text/ appears/2006/05/105546.shtml*.

16. "A Statement Made By Russian President Vladimir Putin on December 13, 2001, Regarding the Decision of the Administration of the United States of America To Withdraw from the Antiballistic Missile Treaty of 1972," December 13, 2001, available from *www.acq.osd.mil/tc/treaties/abm/PutinDec13.htm*.

17. "Remarks By the President on National Missile Defense, ABM Withdrawal," December 13, 2001, available from *www.acq. osd.mil/tc/treaties/abm/remarks.htm*.

18. Toby Harnden, "Secret US deal with Putin over ABM treaty," *Daily Telegraph*, December 14, 2001, available from *www. telegraph.co.uk/news/worldnews/northamerica/usa/1365326/Secret-US-deal-with-Putin-over-ABM-treaty.html*.

19. "Remarks By The President On National Missile Defense, ABM Withdrawal.

20. "U.S. Eyes Missile Defense Site in Europe," Washington, DC: Arms Control Association, July 8, 2004, available from *www. armscontrol.org/act/2004_07-08/MDSite*.

21. Quotations in this section are derived from Keir Giles, "Russian Views on Ballistic Missile Defence in Europe," Shrivenham, Swindon, Wiltshire, UK: Defence Academy of the United Kingdom, Advanced Research and Assessment Group, February 2008.

22. Vanessa Gera And Monika Scislowska, "US, Poland OK Missile Defense Base, Riling Moscow," *Huffington Post*, August

20, 2008, available from *www.huffingtonpost.com/2008/08/20/rice-signs-missile-defens_n_120028.html*.

23. "Central Europe's Leaders Ask Barack Obama to Take Strong Line with Russia," *Daily Telegraph*, July 16, 2009. "An Open Letter to the Obama Administration from Central and Eastern Europe," *Gazeta Wyborcza*, July 16, 2009, available from *wyborcza.pl/1,76842,6825987,An_Open_Letter_to_the_Obama_Administration_from_Central.html*.

24. Peter Baker, "White House Scraps Bush's Approach to Missile Shield," *New York Times*, September 17, 2009, available from *www.nytimes.com/2009/09/18/world/europe/18shield.html?_r=2&hp&*.

25. "Biden Heads To Poland To Mend Relations," CBS News, October 20, 2009, available from *www.cbsnews.com/2100-250_162-5400952.html*.

26. See, for example, "Yesterday Moscow Was Contentedly Rubbing Its Hands, Warsaw and Prague, on the Contrary, Were Wringing Them in Despair," *Moskovskiy Komsomolets*, September 18, 2009.

27. U.S. Department of State website, available from *www.state.gov/t/avc/rls/162447.htm*.

28. BBC Monitoring (BBCM) composite report: "NATO Should Be First to Offer Compromise on Missile Defence—Russian Envoy," July 1, 2011.

29. BBCM: "Russian NATO Envoy Backs Semi-Integrated, Semi-Separate Missile Defence," *RIA-Novosti*, July 1, 2011.

30. BBCM: "Russia's NATO Envoy Accuses Obama's Team of Scuppering ABM Talks," *Rossiya 24* news channel, July 6, 2011.

31. BBCM: "Russian NATO Envoy Backs Semi-Integrated, Semi-Separate Missile Defence."

32. For a review of the A-135 missile defense system, see *missilethreat.com/defense-systems/a-135-abm-3-gazelle/*.

33. Private interview, September 2011.

34. BBCM: "Russia Not to Listen to NATO Head's Advice on Nuclear Weapons—Envoy," *Interfax*, June 16, 2011.

35. "Russia, NATO End Talks on Sectoral Missile Defense—Source," *RIA-Novosti*, July 15, 2011, available from *en.rian.ru/military_news/20110715/165215647.html*.

36. As voiced, for example, by then Russian Chief of General Staff Nikolai Makarov when threatening Finland over its relationship with NATO in June 2012. See "Kenraali Makarovin puhe kokonaisuudessaan" ("General Makarov's Speech In Full"), *Yle news*, June 7, 2012, available from *yle.fi/uutiset/kenraali_makarovin_puhe_kokonaisuudessaan/6169951*.

37. Stephen A. Hildreth and Carl Ek, "Missile Defense and NATO's Lisbon Summit," Washington, DC: Congressional Research Service, January 11, 2011, p. 5 onwards, available from *www.fas.org/sgp/crs/row/R41549.pdf*.

38. "Breaking the 'cold spell' in Russia-NATO Relations," *Russia Today*, November 22, 2010, available from *rt.com/politics/nato-russia-lisbon-summit/*.

39. Keir Giles, "The State of the NATO-Russia Reset," Oxford, UK: Conflict Studies Research Centre, September 2011, p. 20 onwards.

40. *RIA Novosti*'s roundup of reportage from the meeting is available from *en.rian.ru/*.

41. Interview with then Deputy Head of Mission of the Russian Mission to NATO Nikolai Korchunov, June 2011.

42. *Russia Today*, July 4, 2011, available from *rt.com/news/russia-nato-sochi-summit/*.

43. *Deutsche Welle*, July 4, 2011, available from *www.dw.de/russia-warns-nato-over-missile-defense-shield-plans/a-15210166*.

44. *Global Security Newswire*, July 5, 2011, available from *www.nti.org/gsn/article/russia-nato-relations-stuck-on-missile-defense/*.

45. "NATO-Russia Council Makes Progress in Sochi," *NATO website*, July 4, 2011, available from *www.nato.int/cps/en/natolive/news_76039.htm*.

46. Tom Collina, "U.S.-Russia Missile Defense Talks Deadlock," Washington, DC: Arms Control Association, January/February 2012, available from *www.armscontrol.org/act/2012_01-02/US_Russia_Missile_Defense_Talks_Deadlock*.

47. Dmitry Medvedev, "Statement in Connection with the Situation Concerning the NATO Countries' Missile Defence System in Europe," Russian presidential website, November 23, 2011, available from *eng.kremlin.ru/news/3115*.

48. Anders Fogh Rasmussen, "NATO and Russia Can Defend Together," *The New York Times*, December 5, 2011, available from *www.nytimes.com/2011/12/06/opinion/nato-and-russia-can-defend-together.html?_r=0*.

49. Collina.

50. As stated by Deputy Secretary-General Alexander Vershbow at the RUSI Missile Defence Conference, London, UK, June 12, 2013.

51. For example, most recently at the time of writing, as stated on record by Frank Rose (Deputy Assistant Secretary of State for Space and Defense Policy, U.S. Department of State), Nancy Morgan (Director for International Affairs, U.S. Missile Defense Agency), Alexander Vershbow (Deputy Secretary General, NATO) and others at the RUSI Missile Defence Conference, London, UK, June 2013.

52. "Russian Foreign Minister Sergey Lavrov Interview to the Vesti 24 Television Channel, Moscow, July 7, 2011" Russian Ministry of Foreign Affairs website, available from *www.mid.ru/bdomp//brp_4.nsf/english/2FA3CA1205302976C32578C70051B17B*.

53. Remarks at IISS briefing on "US-Russia Relations in Obama's Second Term: Implications for Europe," February 6, 2012, available from *www.iiss.org/en/events/events/archive/2013-5126/february-677e/us-russia-relations-in-obamas-second-term-implications-for-europe-9b92*.

54. Interview, June 2013.

55. BBCM composite report, "Russian Ambassador Says Talks with NATO Didn't Resolve Single Dispute," July 5, 2011.

56. Aleksandr Stukalin, "Missile Defense: Old Problem, No New Solution," Moscow Defense Brief, February 2011, available from *mdb.cast.ru/mdb/2-2011/item4/article1/*.

57. Steven Pifer, "Obama, Medvedev and Missile Defense," Washington, DC: The Brookings Institution, May 20, 2011, available from *www.brookings.edu/opinions/2011/0521_arms_control_pifer.aspx*.

58. Lauri Mälksoo, "International Law in Foreign Policy Documents of the Russian Federation: A Deconstruction," *Diplomaatia*, May 2011.

59. See, for example, "Backgrounder: U.S. Ballistic Missile Defense," Washington, DC: Council on Foreign Relations, available from *www.cfr.org/missile-defense/us-ballistic-missile-defense/p30607*.

60. See, for instance, Stanislav Kozlov, "ЕвроПРО—PRO И KONTRA—Не все так просто, как это может показаться" ("European Missile Defence, Pro and Contra—Not Everything Is As Simple As It Seems"), *Nezavisimoye voyennoye obozreniye*, July 1, 2011, available from *nvo.ng.ru/concepts/2011-07-01/11_europro.html*.

61. As, for instance, highlighting the "extremely low effectiveness" of the GBI program in commentary published by the Russian International Affairs Council. See Kuznetzov, Yesin, Zolotarev, and Rogov, "*Rossiya i SShA na razvilke: initsiativy Obamy i reaktsii Moskvy*" ("Russia and the USA at a Fork in the Road: Obama's Initiatives and Moscow's Reactions"), July 26, 2013, available from *russiancouncil.ru/inner/?id_4=2156*.

62. For representative commentary by Dvorkin in May 2011, available from *www.youtube.com/watch?v=5jO4ukVzTFs*.

63. Transcript in Russian of meeting between then Prime Minister Putin and defence experts in Sarov, Russia, February 24, 2012.

64. Viktor Yesin and Yevgeniy Savostyanov, *"YevroPRO bez mifof i politiki"* ("European Missile Defence Without Myths or Politics"), *Nezavismoye voyennoye obozreniye*, April 13, 2012.

65. Yousaf Butt and Theodore Postol, "Upsetting the Reset: The Technical Basis of Russian Concern Over NATO Missile Defense," FAS Special Report No. 1, Washington, DC: Federation of American Scientists, September 2011.

66. For presentations given publicly by the United States and Russia at this event, see *www.state.gov/t/avc/c52028.htm* and *www.slideshare.net/rusemblon/russian-mod-views-on-nato-missile-defence-in-europe*, respectively.

67. Briefing by Russian Deputy Defence Minister Anatoliy Ivanovich Antonov, Russian Embassy, London, UK, June 20, 2012.

68. Korchunov interview, June 2011.

69. Colonel-General Viktor Yesin, quoted in "Russia's Main Concerns in Talks with U.S., NATO on Missile Defense Systems Have Been Eliminated — Expert," Interfax, March 19, 2013.

70. Anonymous interview, June 2013.

71. See Deputy Defence Minister Antonov quoted in "Russian Defense Ministry Cautiously Optimistic on US Refusal from Missile Shield in Europe" [sic], Interfax, April 5, 2013.

72. "Talks on Further Nuke Cuts Have to Involve Not Only Russia and U.S. — Lavrov," Interfax, June 22, 2013.

73. For a review of the regional threat, see Bruce Klingner, "Missile Defence Requirements of the Asia Pivot," *Defense Dossier*, American Foreign Policy Council, January 2013.

74. Korchunov interview, June 2011.

75. "Russia, USA Cannot Discuss Nuclear Disarmament in Isolation — Official," Interfax, July 25, 2013.

76. For an exploration of how apparently common security terminology in fact masks significant differences in interpretation, see Andrew Monaghan, "The Indivisibility of Security: Russia and Euro-Atlantic Security," Rome, Italy: NATO Defense College, January 2010, available from *www.ndc.nato.int/research/series.php?icode=2.*

77. See the section entitled "A Predictive Case Study: How President Vladimir Putin and His Successors Might Reasonably Expect Nuclear Devaluation to Endanger Their Strategic Future," Paul Schulte, "The Strategic Risks of Devaluing Nuclear Weapons," *Contemporary Security Policy*, Vol. 34, No. 1, 2013, pp. 195-220.

78. The comment is widely attributed to German Chancellor Helmut Schmidt in the late-1980s.

79. E. Wayne Merry, "Ballistic Missile Defense Through Russian Eyes," *Defense Dossier*, American Foreign Policy Council, January 2013.

80. *Ibid.*

81. BBCM: "Russian Envoy Still Hopes to "Persuade" NATO on Missile Defence," *Rossiya 1 TV*, July 9, 2011.

82. Heidi Reisinger, "A NATO transit hub in Ulyanovsk — What's behind the Russian debate?" Rome, Italy: NATO Defense College, April 2012, available from *www.ndc.nato.int/research/series.php?icode=3.*

83. Conference proceedings, "The Changing Nature of Ballistic Missile Defense," Washington, DC: National Defense University, June 3-4, 2009.

84. As quoted in "Waking the Neighbour: Finland, NATO and Russia," Shrivenham, Swindon, Wiltshire, UK: UK Defence Academy, September 2009.

85. See Keir Giles, "The Military Doctrine of the Russian Federation 2010," Rome, Italy: NATO Defense College, February 2010, available from *www.academia.edu/343489/The_Military_Doctrine_of_the_Russian_Federation_2010.*

86. I. Yu. Yurgens and S. A. Kulik, eds., "*O perspektivakh razvitiya otnosheniy Rossii i NATO*" ("*On prospects for development of relations between Russia and NATO*"), Institut sovremennogo razvitiya (INSOR), October 2010, pp. 38-41.

87. Andrei Fedyashin, "Russia and NATO Agree to Wait until Chicago," *RIA-Novosti*, July 5, 2011, available from *en.rian.ru/analysis/20110705/165028339.html.*

88. Sarov meeting transcript, February 24, 2012.

89. As echoed, in fact, by Postol and Butt, p. 30.

90. See for example, most recently, Aleksey Arbatov and Vladimir Dvorkin, "*Voyennaya reforma Rossii: sostoyaniye i perspektivy*" ("Russia's Military Reform: Status and Prospects"), Moscow, Russia: Carnegie Moscow Centre, 2013.

91. Keir Giles, Russian Military Transformation: Goal in Sight? Carlisle Barracks, PA: Strategic Studies Institute, U.S. Army War College, May 5, 2014.

92. As detailed in briefings to NATO by the Russian General Staff Academy, November 2012.

93. CCTN News in English, available from *english.cntv.cn/program/newsupdate/20130621/102936.shtml.*

94. "Putin: Be Aware of Plans for First Strike Capability," LarouchePAC, June 21, 2013, available from *larouchepac.com/node/27054.*

95. Speaking at the RUSI Missile Defence Conference, June 2013.

96. Matthew Bunn, "Foundation for the Future: The ABM Treaty and National Security," Washington, DC: Arms Control Association, 1990, p. 87.

97. BBCM: "Russia's NATO Envoy Accuses Obama's Team of Scuppering ABM Talks."

98. "Russia Hardens Its Position on Plans to Build Anti-Missile Shield," *Eastweek*, May 18, 2011, available from *www.osw. waw.pl/en/publikacje/analyses/2011-05-18/russia-hardens-its-position-plans-to-build-anti-missile-shield*.

99. BBCM: "Russia Sets No Deadlines to Resolve US Missile Defence Disagreements—Minister," *RIA-Novosti*, July 12, 2011.

100. BBCM: "Russian Envoy Still Hopes to "Persuade" NATO on Missile Defence."

101. Korchunov interview, June 2011.

102. Aleksandr Gabuyev, "Ваш сектор возле Russia" [sic] ("Your Sector Opposite Russia"), *Kommersant*, July 16, 2011, available from *www.kommersant.ru/doc/1680689/print*.

103. Medvedev, "Statement in Connection with the Situation Concerning the NATO Countries' Missile Defence System in Europe."

104. "Missile Defense: Toward a New Paradigm," EASI Working Group on Missile Defense, Washington, DC: Carnegie Endowment for International Peace, February 2012, available from *carnegieendowment.org/2012/02/03/missile-defense-toward-new-paradigm/9cvz*.

105. Private interview, May 2013.

106. Peter B. Doran, "EPAA Phase Four: Avoiding Death by a Thousand Cuts," Washington, DC: Center for European Policy Analysis, March 20, 2013, available from *www.cepa.org/sites/default/files/documents/CEPA%20Op-ed,%20EPAA%20Phase%20Four.pdf*.

107. "US-Russia Relations and the Asia-Pacific," London, UK: IISS, July 26, 2013, available from *www.iiss.org/en/events/events/archive/2013-5126/july-bdc1/us-russia-relations-and-the-asia-pacific-7097.*

108. "European Security: Russian Proposals," Shrivenham, Swindon, Wiltshire, UK: Advanced Research and Assessment Group, Defence Academy of the United Kingdom, January 2009.

109. Keir Giles, "The Nature of the Georgian Ceasefire," Shrivenham, Swindon, Wiltshire, UK: Advanced Research and Assessment Group, Defence Academy of the United Kingdom, August 13, 2008.

110. See Morten Langsholdt, "Russia and the Use of Force: Theory and Practice,", Report 2005/02504, Kjeller, Norway: Norwegian Defence Research Establishment November 2005, available from *www.ffi.no/no/Rapporter/05-02504.pdf.*

111. For a detailed examination of the Iskander system, including its role in the BMD debate, see Stefan Forss, "The Russian Operational-Tactical Iskander Missile System," Working Papers No. 42, Helsinki, Finland: Finnish National Defence University Department of Strategic and Defence Studies, 2012.

112. "Russia Deploys S-400 Missile Defense in Kaliningrad," *Novinite*, April 7, 2012, available from *www.novinite.com/view_news.php?id=138312.*

113. Aleksey Arbatov, "Look Before You Leap," *Nezavisimoye Voyennoye Obozreniye*, August 2, 2013.

114. Pavel Tarasenko, "*Rossiya i NATO soshlis na vertoletakh i borbe s terrorismom*" ("Russia and NATO Come Together on Helicopters and Counter-Terrorism"), *Kommersant*, April 24, 2013, p. 7.

115. "Putin Letter to Obama to Address Missile Defense, Security," *RIA-Novosti*, May 15, 2013, available from *en.rian.ru/russia/20130515/181170446.html.*

116. "Russian Foreign Minister Sergey Lavrov Interview to the Vesti 24 Television Channel, Moscow, July 7, 2011" Russian Ministry of Foreign Affairs website, available from *www.mid.ru/ brp_4.nsf/0/2FA3CA1205302976C32578C70051B17B.*

117. Anonymous interview, July 2013.

118. Anonymous interview, June 2013.

119. "Concept of the Foreign Policy of the Russian Federation," approved February 12, 2013, available in English from *www.mid.ru/bdomp/brp_4.nsf/e78a48070f128a7b43256999005bcbb3/7 6389fec168189ed44257b2e0039b16d!OpenDocument.*

120. Merry.